Children's

GOURMET

Gifts

Children's
G O U R M E T
Gifts

*Beautiful projects for children
and adults to create together*

To my husband for

his unwavering support,

my children for their

daily inspiration, and

my parents for

believing in me.

Published by Marcia Porch
Copyright 2001
ISBN: 0-9704503-0-3
LC Control Number: 00-092754

Edited, designed, and manufactured by
Favorite Recipes® Press
An imprint of

FRP

2451 Atrium Way
Nashville, Tennessee 37214
1-800-358-0560

Printed in Mexico

First Printing: 2001   5,000 copies

To order additional copies of this book,
please call 1-800-358-0560

Book Design: Jim Scott
Art Director: Steve Newman
Project Manager: Ginger Dawson

Photography by: Roberto Gonzolez

Introduction

For the past ten years I have had the honor of teaching children's cooking classes. With every class, I continue to be amazed by their unique abilities. Each child truly has a limitless imagination waiting to be unleashed. One of the most popular areas of my classes has been gifts the children have made for others. This book was designed as an opportunity for them (with adult help) to create beautiful gifts for relatives, teachers, neighbors, and friends. The goal of each recipe is to maximize creativity and foster a tremendous sense of accomplishment. Recipes range from simple mixes any child can measure into an attractive cellophane bag or jar to more complex decorating projects. Below is the key for the ease of the recipes.

 **easy**

 **medium**

 **advanced**

Table of Contents

Marzipan Ducks

This recipe may be used to create a variety of adorable shapes.
Try making chicks, bunnies, teddy bears, mice and more.
Have fun and use your imagination!

$^1/_2$ pound (8 ounces) almond paste
2 tablespoons light corn syrup
1$^1/_2$ cups confectioners' sugar, sifted
Yellow food color
Red food color
Black gel food color or chocolate icing

1 Combine the almond paste and corn syrup in a large mixing bowl. Add the confectioners' sugar gradually, mixing until just blended. Divide the mixture into walnut-size pieces. Shape into balls.

2 Shape into a duck by gently pulling a small amount to form the neck and head and curve the remaining large part to form the body. Make indentations for the duck's eyes and feathers using a wooden pick. Combine 2 teaspoons of water and 6 drops of yellow food color in a small bowl. Paint the ducks body yellow using a small paintbrush.

3 Combine 1 teaspoon of water, 3 drops of yellow food color and 3 drops of red food color in a small bowl. Paint the ducks beaks orange using a small paintbrush. Dot eyes on the duck using a wooden pick dipped in the black gel food color or chocolate icing.

Shortcuts: For maximum ease, use prepackaged marzipan
and follow the directions above for shaping and coloring.
Make ducks in several sizes to create a duck family.

Chocolate Kitty Truffles

YIELD: 35 TO 40 KITTIES

Include a box of real kitty treats and a toy for your favorite cat lover and their cat!

12 ounces (2 cups) semisweet chocolate chips
3/4 cup (6 ounces) sweetened condensed milk
1 teaspoon instant coffee granules
1/2 teaspoon salt
2 teaspoons vanilla extract
1 (14-ounce) package chocolate candy melting disks
2 to 3 teaspoons vegetable oil
1/2 bag white chocolate chips

1 Melt the chocolate chips in a microwave-safe bowl at 50% power, stirring after each minute until smooth. Add the condensed milk and mix well. Thoroughly combine the coffee granules, salt and vanilla in a small bowl. Whisk into the chocolate mixture until well blended. Chill at least 1 hour. Divide the mixture into walnut-size pieces and shape into balls. Pinch the top of each ball and create 2 pointed kitty ears.

2 Melt the chocolate candy disks in a microwave-safe bowl at 50% power, stirring after each minute. Add the vegetable oil 1 teaspoon at a time, whisking until smooth and the mixture pours easily. Dip each kitty into the chocolate mixture with a fork. You may need to spoon additional mixture over the kitty to completely coat it. Tap the fork lightly on the side of the bowl to remove the excess. Place the chocolate-coated kitties on foil sheets or a wire rack. If the chocolate mixture begins to cool, reheat in the microwave to make the dipping easier.

3 Melt the white chocolate chips in a microwave-safe bowl at 50% power, stirring after each minute. Paint white chocolate eyes and whiskers on each kitty using a small paintbrush or a wooden pick dipped in the melted white chocolate. Let dry for 1 hour or more.

Shortcuts: Make the truffle centers ahead. Shape into a ball after chilling the mixture for 1 hour. Return to the refrigerator and chill for up to 1 week until you are ready to finish them.

Caramel Popcorn Hands

YIELD: ABOUT 4 HANDS

 (with store-bought popcorn)

For a really authentic look, purchase inexpensive plastic rings,
bracelets and bugs from a party store and decorate each hand accordingly.
These are a great hit for a class or party!

1 bag plain microwave popcorn, popped
2 cups cashews (or other favorite nut)
1 cup (2 sticks) butter
2 cups packed brown sugar
1/2 cup light corn syrup
1 teaspoon salt
1/2 teaspoon baking soda
1 1/2 teaspoons vanilla extract
Jelly beans
Clear plastic gloves

1 Combine the popcorn and cashews in a large roasting pan. Melt the butter in a large saucepan on the stove. Stir in the brown sugar, corn syrup and salt. Bring to a boil, stirring constantly. Place a candy thermometer on the side of the pan and boil for 5 minutes, without stirring, until the temperature reaches 250 degrees.

2 Remove from the heat and stir in the baking soda and vanilla. Pour over the popcorn and cashews, mixing to coat well. Bake at 225 degrees for 1 hour, stirring twice during baking.

3 Let cool and break into pieces small enough to fit into the plastic gloves. Place 3 jelly beans into each finger of the glove to resemble fingernails. Fill the glove with the caramel corn and tie the top of the glove with lots of ribbon.

Shortcuts: For maximum ease, purchase prepackaged caramel nut popcorn and fill the gloves as directed above. You will need **2** cups of popcorn for each hand. You may purchase the clear plastic gloves at a restaurant supply store.

Herbes de Provence Rice Mix

YIELD: 6 TO 8 SERVINGS

Place the cellophane bag inside a decorative rice bowl for a pretty gift.

1¹/₂ cups rice
1 tablespoon chicken bouillon granules
1 tablespoon dried minced onion
1 teaspoon dried basil
1 teaspoon dried rosemary
1 teaspoon dried thyme

 Combine the rice, bouillon granules, dried onion, basil, rosemary and thyme in a large bowl and mix well. You may crush the spices between your fingers as they are added to increase the flavor.

 Spoon into a colorful cellophane bag and tie with ribbon. You may also pour into a jar with a tight-fitting lid. Tie the following preparation directions on the package or place a label on the back of the bag.

Directions

3 cups water
1 tablespoon butter
Herbes de Provence Rice Mix

 Bring the water and butter to a boil in a medium saucepan on the stove. Add the rice mix and reduce the heat to simmer. Cover and cook for 15 to 20 minutes until the water has evaporated and the rice is fluffy.

Shortcuts: Assemble a row of open bags or jars and measure one recipe into each bag if you need several mixes.

Best Snack Mix

YIELD: 18 CUPS

 (need oven) (pictured on page 14)

Let children decorate white Chinese take-out cartons to create fun gift containers. These are available at party stores.

1 cup (2 sticks) butter, melted
1 tablespoon Worcestershire sauce
1 teaspoon chili powder
1 teaspoon garlic powder
6 cups corn chips or sesame sticks
2½ cups whole cashews
4 cups cheddar fish-shaped crackers
6 cups popped popcorn (approximately 1 microwaved bag)
2 cups pecan halves

1 Combine the melted butter, Worcestershire sauce, chili powder and garlic powder in a bowl and mix well. Measure the corn chips, cashews, fish crackers, popcorn and pecans in a large roasting pan and blend together.

2 Pour the butter mixture over the corn chip mixture, stirring to coat well. Bake at 250 degrees for 1 hour, stirring 2 or 3 times to evenly distribute the ingredients. Spoon the mixture onto paper towels and let cool. Package in cellophane bags tied with ribbon or metal tins.

Suggestions: This recipe will make several bags, so it is terrific to give as teacher or neighbor gifts. If you do not have a large roasting pan, divide the dry ingredients into **2** smaller pans and pour half of the butter mixture over each one.

Farfalle Chicken Soup Mix

YIELD: 4 SERVINGS

 (pictured on page 14)

Place the decorated cellophane bag of this comforting soup
inside a pretty soup bowl for a special gift.

2 cups farfalle (bowtie) pasta
1 tablespoon plus 1 teaspoon chicken bouillon granules
1 tablespoon dried minced onion
1 teaspoon garlic powder

1 Combine the pasta, bouillon granules, dried onion and garlic powder in a bowl and mix well. Pour the mixture into a decorative cellophane bag and tie with a matching ribbon. Place a label on the back of the bag or attach the following preparation directions with a ribbon.

Directions

5 cups water
Farfalle Chicken Soup Mix
1 cup (or more) chopped cooked chicken (optional)

2 Bring the water to a boil in a medium saucepan on the stove. Add the soup mix and boil gently for 12 minutes or until the pasta tests done. Stir in the chicken for extra heartiness. Serve immediately.

Shortcuts: Assemble a row of open bags and measure
one recipe into each bag for multiple gifts. Attach the
preparation directions with colorful ribbon.

Decorated Dipped Stirring Spoons

YIELD: 35 TO 40 SPOONS

You may purchase lollipop bags in a candy or crafts store. Place the dipped end of the spoon into each bag and tie with ribbon for an especially polished look.

6 ounces chocolate candy melting disks
35 to 40 clear plastic teaspoons
Decorating sugar or candy sprinkles

1 Place the chocolate candy disks in a microwave-safe bowl. Microwave at 50% power, stirring after 1 minute. Repeat until the disks are melted smoothly. Dip the entire top of the spoons into the melted chocolate. Tap the spoon lightly on the side of the bowl to remove the excess.

2 Place on baking sheets lined with foil or parchment paper to let dry. If the chocolate mixture begins to cool, reheat in the microwave to make the dipping easier. Sprinkle with the decorating sugar or coat with candy sprinkles before the chocolate dries completely. You may purchase the clear plastic teaspoons at a party supply store.

Suggestions: Wrap a group of spoons in cellophane and tie with sparkling ribbon and place in a mug. This makes a great gift for any family member, friend or teacher.

Comfy Hot Cocoa Mix

YIELD: 11 SERVINGS

You may multiply this recipe according to the number of gifts you need to make.

²/₃ cup sugar
¹/₂ cup baking cocoa
1 vanilla bean pod
3 cups instant dry milk

 Combine the sugar and baking cocoa in a bowl and stir together. Cut the vanilla bean lengthwise and gently scrape out the inside seeds. Mash the vanilla seeds with the back of a spoon into the sugar mixture. Add the dry milk and mix well.

 Pour into a large decorative jar or divide into 2 smaller jars to give as gifts. Also you may pour into cellophane bags tied with ribbon. Be sure to include the following preparation directions.

Directions

 Combine ¹/₃ cup Comfy Hot Cocoa Mix with 8 ounces of hot water. Mix well until cocoa mixture is dissolved. Top with marshmallows and enjoy!

Suggestions: Place a cellophane bag of cocoa mix
inside a pretty mug for a very special gift.

Mulled Cider with a Twist Mix

YIELD: 10 SERVINGS

 (pictured on page 20)

Tie the cellophane wrapped bag to a bottle of apple cider for an attractive gift.
Write the preparation directions on a large label and attach to
the back of the apple cider bottle.

**1 teaspoon whole allspice
1 teaspoon whole cloves
4 small cinnamon sticks
1 whole nutmeg seed
Cheesecloth (12×12-inch square)**

1 Combine the allspice, cloves, cinnamon sticks and nutmeg seed in a small bowl. Place in the center of the cheesecloth square. Tie the cheesecloth ends in a knot or tie with string to make a little bag. Place in a cellophane bag and tie with colorful ribbon. Attach the following preparation directions.

Directions

**2 quarts apple cider or apple juice
2 cups orange juice
2/3 cup packed brown sugar
Mulled Cider with a Twist Mix**

2 Combine the apple cider, orange juice and brown sugar in a large saucepan on the stove, stirring until the brown sugar is dissolved. Add the cheesecloth bag to the cider mixture. Bring to a boil. Reduce the heat and let simmer for 15 minutes. Pour into mugs to serve. Garnish with an orange slice twist.

Shortcuts: This is a great recipe to make if you need many gifts. The ingredients are inexpensive and the cheesecloth bags may be assembled quickly. Try buying cinnamon sticks in bulk, which are found in many ethnic markets.

☆Orange Spiced Tea Mix

YIELD: 25 SERVINGS

 (pictured on page 20)

Place the cellophane bag filled with mix in a colorful mug,
tie with ribbon and give as a gift.

**2 cups orange breakfast drink mix
$^1/_2$ cup instant tea mix
1 cup sugar
1 teaspoon cinnamon
$^1/_2$ teaspoon ground cloves**

1 Combine the orange drink mix, instant tea mix, sugar, cinnamon and cloves in a medium bowl and mix well. Pour into a decorative jar with a tight-fitting lid or 2 cellophane bags tied with ribbon. Attach the following preparation directions with a label on the back or with a ribbon.

Directions

2 Combine 2 tablespoons of the Orange Spiced Tea Mix and 8 ounces of hot water in a mug. Stir until the mix is dissolved. This is also great served over ice.

Shortcuts: This is an easy recipe that may be doubled, tripled or more to produce multiple gifts.

Charming Cookie Bouquets

YIELD: 32 FLOWER COOKIES

 (need oven)

Write the children's name in the center of each cookie flower with the icing.

**Scrumptious Sugar Cookies (page 26) or
1 (18-ounce) package refrigerated sugar cookie dough
30 (8-inch) lollipop sticks
Butter Icing (page 25) or purchased yellow decorating icing
Chocolate Icing (page 25)
Green floral tape
Small green paper napkins
Styrofoam blocks or green florist's foam blocks
Colored tissue paper
Bright colored ribbon**

1 Remove the plastic package from the cookie dough. Slice the dough into 8 equal portions. Cut each portion into 4 pieces and shape each piece into a ball. Insert a lollipop stick into each cookie dough ball. Place on an ungreased cookie sheet, pressing down lightly to form a circle.

2 Bake at 350 degrees for 10 minutes. You will only be able to bake 4 to 6 cookies at one time because the lollipop sticks are long. Be careful to not let the cookies touch. Remove to a wire rack to let the cookies cool. Decorate with the Butter Icing and Chocolate Icing to make a sunflower.

Suggestions: You may create one large basket bouquet of cookies for a class or party.

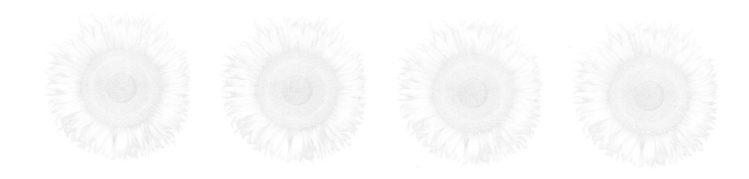

Butter Icing

½ cup (1 stick) butter, softened
1 (1-pound) box confectioners' sugar
2 to 3 tablespoons milk
1 teaspoon vanilla extract
Yellow food color

 Beat the butter in a mixing bowl until light and fluffy. Add the confectioners' sugar gradually, beating until well blended. Add the milk gradually, beating until of spreading consistency. Mix in the vanilla and desired amount of food color. Spoon the icing into a sealable plastic bag. Cut a very small corner off of the bottom of the bag. Squeeze the icing through to decorate petals on each cookie.

Chocolate Icing

 Purchase prepared chocolate icing from a grocery store. Spoon into a sealable plastic bag. Cut a very small corner off of the bottom of the bag. Squeeze the icing through to make small dots in the center of each cookie to resemble seeds.

Bouquet

YIELD: 8 BOUQUETS

 Wrap the lollipop stick with green floral tape. Tape the green paper napkin on the stick to resemble flower leaves and cover with more floral tape if desired. Insert 4 or 5 cookie flowers into the styrofoam block. Cover the foam block with colorful tissue paper and tie with the ribbon.

Scrumptious Sugar Cookies

YIELD: 32 COOKIES

 (need oven)

$^1/_2$ **cup (1 stick) butter, softened**
1 cup sugar
1 egg
1 teaspoon vanilla extract
2 cups flour
1 teaspoon baking powder
$^1/_2$ **teaspoon salt**

1 Beat the butter and sugar in a large mixing bowl until light and fluffy. Add the egg and vanilla and mix well. Stir in the flour, baking powder and salt just until blended. Wrap the cookie dough in plastic wrap and chill for at least 30 minutes.

2 Divide the dough into 30 walnut-size pieces. Shape pieces into balls. Follow the directions on page 24 to make the cookie flower bouquets.

Cookie Champions

YIELD: 48 COOKIE MEDALS

 (need oven)

These are ideal for a class or team party.

1 cup creamy peanut butter
1 cup (2 sticks) butter, softened
1 cup packed brown sugar
1 cup sugar
2 eggs
1 teaspoon vanilla extract
3 cups flour
2 teaspoons baking soda
Chocolate icing (purchased at a grocery store)
Candy sprinkles and ribbon

 Beat the peanut butter, butter, brown sugar and sugar in a large mixing bowl until well blended. Add the eggs and vanilla. Sift the flour and baking soda together and mix in just until blended. Divide the dough into 48 walnut-size pieces. Shape into balls. Arrange 6 each on ungreased cookie sheets. Flatten with the bottom of a glass that has been dipped in sugar. Make a hole in the top of each cookie using a straw.

 Bake at 350 degrees for 8 to 10 minutes. You may use a straw to define the hole in the top of the cookies if it closes slightly during baking. Remove to a wire rack to cool completely.

To make the cookie medals, spoon the chocolate icing into a sealable plastic bag. Cut a very small corner off of the bottom of the bag. Squeeze the icing through to outline each cookie and write a saying in the center. Decorate with the candy sprinkles. Let the icing dry. Thread the ribbon through the hole in the cookie and tie a knot in the end.

Shortcuts: For a big timesaver, use peanut butter cookie mix purchased at a grocery store. Follow the directions above for baking.

29

Memories & Notes